OH *Beautiful* BEER

The Evolution of Craft Beer & Design

Harvey Shepard

The Countryman Press

A division of W. W. Norton & Company

Independent Publishers Since 1923

The Countryman Press
www.countrymanpress.com

A division of W. W. Norton & Company, Inc.
500 Fifth Avenue, New York, NY 10110
www.wwnorton.com

For information about permission to
reproduce selections from this book,
write to Permissions, W. W. Norton & Company, Inc.,
500 Fifth Avenue, New York, NY 10110

For information about special discounts for bulk
purchases, please contact W. W. Norton Special Sales
at specialsales@wwnorton.com or 800-233-4830

978-1-58157-315-2

1 2 3 4 5 6 7 8 9 0

To Leah, for her appreciation of good beer, clean design, and me

Contents

1 | The Beginning

Beer has been around for thousands of years, so it should come as no surprise that we have found many different ways to deliver it to our mouths. The early evolution of beer drinking vessels is a long list that includes skulls, cattle horns, steins, mugs, tankards, and cups. Stoneware, ceramics, pewter, wood, leather, bronze, silver, gold, porcelain, and china have all been used extensively as the base materials.

For a long time, bars and breweries were undoubtedly the favorite place to enjoy a beer. This trend began to turn after Prohibition, as take-home packaging started to hit its stride and consumers began drinking at home more commonly.

Historically, beer labels have not always matched the contents of the bottles on which they appeared. It was once common practice for lesser brewers to sell forgeries of popular beers and brews marketed as "imports" were often actually produced locally. These techniques were especially problematic for popular brewers Guinness, William Younger, and Bass. Low quality imposters sold under their names were diminishing their brands.

On January 1, 1876, a solution for these breweries arrived in the form of the United Kingdom's Trade Marks Registration Act. Wanting to be the first to take advantage of this new legislation, Bass sent an employee to wait outside the registrar's office overnight. For their efforts, Bass's Red Triangle became the world's first registered trademark. Bass also received trademark number two, the Red Diamond, for their strong ale.

Design credits: Bauhaus Brew Labs by Helms Workshop, Bottle Logic by Emrich Office, Brown's Brewing by id29, Daredevil Brewing by Cultivator Advertising & Design, Fair State by Little & Company, Fullsteam by Helms Workshop, Great Divide by Cultivator Advertising & Design, Great Raft by Derouen & Co., Partizan Brewing by Alec Doherty, Sixpoint Brewery by Lefty Lexington

St. Peter's Brewery

BUNGAY, ENGLAND • DESIGN BY NELSON ASSOCIATES

People began experimenting with beer in glass bottles as far back as the 16th century. Like other alcoholic beverages, it was put into hand-blown glass bottles affixed with a cork. The high-pressured nature of beer caused this situation to be less than ideal. It was accidentally discovered that beer left in a bottle underwent a secondary fermentation, causing an explosive increase in carbonation. Thicker bottles were called into duty and corks were reinforced with twine and wire. Beer in glass bottles would not become commercially available for another hundred years.

Advances in manufacturing, as well England lifting the glass tax in 1845, paved the way for beer bottles to thrive in the market. The discovery of pasteurization in 1876 was a major victory for beer bottles, as breweries now had a way to keep bottled beer fresh for much longer. This discovery coincided with the growth of the American rail system, together sparking a boom in distribution.

While time and technology has left these early bottles behind, St. Peter's Brewery sought to revive them. Despite opening in England in 1997, they found their inspiration in 18th century America.

These distinctive oval, high-shouldered bottles are a replica of a gin bottle found outside of Philadelphia. This bottle dated back to 1770 and was produced for local innkeeper Thomas Gerrard.

While so many breweries stand out for their iconic artwork, Nelson Associates focused the brand around the bottle itself. They created a sophisticated and subtle labeling approach. Free of paper, the bottle is embossed with the brewery's logo and details about the beer are spelled out in gold foil lettering, which is applied directly to the bottle.

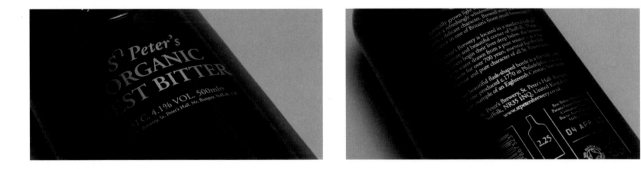

Rogue

NEWPORT, OREGON, USA • DESIGN BY PENNY MUIRE

Beginning in the mid-19th century, ceramic was a popular choice for beer bottles, especially porters. These vessels were strong, heavy, and expensive to produce. Thus, breweries took extra measures to encourage their return, embossing their name and city across the bottle. If the company also produced soft drinks, words like "Beer Co." would be omitted. This style mostly disappeared with the 1800s.

Rogue's XS series pays homage to these relics, with a range of strong ales packaged in ceramic swing-top 750ml bottles. These Rogue bottles are rather popular with homebrewers. As bootleggers in the 1800s quickly realized, these are ideal for refilling with a libation of your own.

Up until bottles became popular (and practical) in the early 1900s, the only way to bring beer home was by the bucketful. Fresh beer was filled at the local bar and carried home in "growlers." These containers were typically two-quart galvanized pails, but could also be pitchers, jars, jugs, or other pieces of pottery. A trip to the bar to refill these buckets was commonly referred to as "rushing the growler" and was performed by children as well as adults.

The history behind the word "growler" has led to some debate. One belief is that while the beer was in transit, the carbon dioxide growled as it escaped underneath the lid of the bucket. Others point to the growling between patrons and bartenders over what constituted a full bucket as the source of the term. Regardless of where the name comes from, that little bucket was just one early step toward the beer packaging we are now accustomed to taking home.

Lucky Bucket Brewing

LA VISTA, NEBRASKA, USA • DESIGN BY ARCHRIVAL

The lucky, beer-filled buckets consumers hauled home during the late 19th and early 20th centuries inspired a beer brand a century later. The founders of this Nebraskan brewery admired the work that it took to enjoy a quality beer at home and their name pays homage to those days.

In 2008, Lucky Bucket began brewing their first batches of Lucky Bucket Pre-Prohibition Style Lager. This brew harkens back to a time when additive-free lagers had flavor and character.

2 | European Beer (& Design) Spread

During the 19th century, many European beer styles spread to the United States as immigrants opened breweries. The packaging reflected just as much of their home as the beer styles they brought with them. Blackletter typography became, and still is, very popular for company logos. Heraldry elements also became quite popular. This trend dates back to when customers brought their own bottles to be filled at breweries, which they often marked with their family coat of arms to claim ownership.

In today's market, we see that these European design elements are still very prominent for breweries crafting German or British beer styles all over the world. Just as the brewers are putting their own spin on the beers, a modern approach is often taken on these design themes that date back several centuries.

Grimm Brothers Brewhouse

LOVELAND, COLORADO, USA • DESIGN BY EMRICH OFFICE

Many breweries use their visual brand to tell their own story. Instead, this Colorado brewery decided to use it put a spin on tales that have been told for hundreds of years.

The founders of Grimm Brothers Brewhouse were fascinated by the long, rich history of German brewing. They committed themselves to properly producing storied beer styles including bocks, dunkel lagers, and alt bier. Another long-lived German tradition is that of storytelling. The Brothers Grimm famously dedicated their lives to collecting and publishing German folklore during the 19th century. Their tales have since been extremely popular and are now available in over a hundred languages and many film adaptions.

Now their fables are also available in liquid form. Their characters have been paired with beer releases from Grimm Brothers Brewhouse. Local designer Josh Emrich has created an enchanting world for these characters to live in. Just as the Grimm Brothers brewers are presenting modern versions of historical beer styles, Emrich's illustrations present contemporary renditions of this cast.

Hilliard's Beer

SEATTLE, WASHINGTON, USA • DESIGN BY MINT DESIGN

These sixteen-ounce cans manage to smoothly blend Old World European design elements into a package that feels straight out of 1960s America. Mint Design crafted a custom blackletter logomark, modernizing a script that dates back to the 12th century. The hard angles of the lettering are echoed in the alternating chevrons that appear on each beer.

Though enjoying a much more recent boom in popularity, the chevron pattern traces back to at least 1800 BC Greek pottery carvings. It also frequently appears in heraldry as one of the main design components of coats of arms. Here, the geometric pattern moves your eye up and down these perfectly uncluttered tallboys.

Their Pacific Northwest take on an amber ale is well hopped, appealing to the region's IPA enthusiasts. The canned saison aims to make the style more accessible. No spices are added, but the brew picks up notes of citrus, peppercorn, and coriander from the Belgian yeast.

Hopworks Urban Brewery • Portland, Oregon, USA • Design by Jolby & Friends

Shiner

SHINER, TEXAS, USA • DESIGN BY MCGARRAH JESSEE

In 1909 the Shiner Brewing Association opened in Shiner, Texas. Six years later, German immigrant Kosmos Spoetzl bought the company, renaming it Spoetzl Brewery. The Bavarian beer recipe Kosmos brought with him to America would soon become Shiner Premium Beer.

At the end of the day, the German and Czech cotton farmers of Shiner would find bottles of Shiner Premium on fence posts strategically placed by Kosmos. This helped make the beer an immediate local favorite.

Spoetzl was one of five Texas breweries to survive

Prohibition. It is rumored that the brewery did so by continuing to brew real beer for the locals who came in to "get some ice."

The refreshed Shiner premium packaging created by McGarrah Jessee embraces the heritage of Spoetzl Brewery, complete with the cotton ball label as a tribute to those immigrant farmers.

When it came time to overhaul the packaging for the famed Shiner Bock, they preserved many of its original design elements. The familiar reds and yellows remained, as did the beer's iconic ram. The prominent blackletter typography and "Prosit!" exclamation keep the brewery's European roots in the forefront.

Brewery advertising does not commonly showcase employees, but Shiner Beer does just that in this series of posters. Several of their fifty-five dedicated employees are featured, showing the passion they have for the product they produce in their tiny hometown of Shiner, Texas.

Brewery Ommegang

COOPERSTOWN, NEW YORK, USA • DESIGN BY DUFFY & PARTNERS

Belgian-style Brewery Ommegang recognized that they were in need of a rebrand. Consumers were enjoying Hennepin, but not associating it with Ommegang and their other offerings. The brewery turned to Duffy & Partners in 2012 to establish a cohesive visual brand. The firm created a successful identity system which clearly ties together the entire Ommegang family of beers. Key brand elements—such as the lion and plaid pattern—survived the rebranding process, making the new look less jarring to customers.

Each beer is carefully crafted in the Belgian style and named with inspiration from various Belgian and local sources. The labels include silhouettes hinting at the story behind each bottle.

Now best known for its Baseball Hall of Fame, Cooperstown was once crowded with hop houses and fields. Hop farms are slowly making a comeback in the area, including one at the brewery that was planted in 2013. Belgian and American hops blend together in this citrusy and tropical pale ale. The rest of the Ommegang lineup is much maltier, including their Abbey Ale. This Belgian Dubbel is brewed in the traditional trappist style, featuring rich spices and deep fruity notes. At 8.2% ABV, their flagship may just make you dance along with the label's monks.

The fox and bird on the amber ale's label are a bit more subdued. Rare Vos (Flemish for "Sly Fox") is named after the Brussels pub famous for its bicycling contests and pigeon races.

Hennepin is a spicy saison named for Father Louis Hennepin. Born in what is now Hainaut, Belgium, Hennepin was the first European to see Niagara Falls. Ommegang's Witte is the perfect reward after a long day of international exploring (or working the wheat fields).

Ommegang's Three Philosophers is a quadruple ale which shares a name with a Giorgione painting from the

Italian High Renaissance. This piece portrays one young, one middle-aged, and one old philosopher. The beer is a blend of 98% Belgian-style dark ale and 2% Liefmans Kriek and results in a high-alcohol masterpiece with notes of dark fruits, molasses and chocolate. Its complexity makes Three Philosophers the perfect beer for contemplation.

The characters gracing the Gnomegang Blonde Ale label are a nod to Belgium's famed Brasserie D'Achouffe ("Chouffe" translates to "gnome"). This beer is brewed with Chouffe fruity signature house yeast and is their only year-round collaboration offering.

Kings Craft Brewing Co.

CAPE TOWN, SOUTH AFRICA • DESIGN BY MONDAY DESIGN

This flagship release from Kings Craft Brewing Company reaches back to 12th century England for inspiration. LionHeart Lager honors King Richard I, whose fearlessness in battle led to the nickname "Richard the Lionheart." Gold details are a perfect fit for this golden lager. A restricted color palette and a simple, stylized crown gives the brand a modern regality. LionHeart features Saaz hops, which are especially popular for Czech-style lagers and pilsners, guaranteeing the beer will have a finish as crisp as the artwork.

Citizen Beer

CAPE TOWN, SOUTH AFRICA • DESIGN BY MONDAY DESIGN

The Citizen Beer artwork feels like more of a uniform than a label. Each beer's name commands attention in large, masculine typography. The style is clearly differentiated by the uniquely colored sashes draped across each label. The line art shield is the centerpiece of the brand, invoking a sense of nobility and a strong link to history. The soft curves of this unusual label shape give the overall look an added elegance. These elements, combined with the "Made with Honour" tagline pay homage to the legacy of beer making.

Shepherd Neame

FAVERSHAM, KENT, ENGLAND • DESIGN BY STUART ADAMS

Early European beer labels were simple shapes and used few colors. Ovular labels dominated the English market, frequently with a thick band across the center displaying the brand or beer name.

Shepherd Neame, Britain's oldest brewery, is a prime example of this oval label theme. These simple shapes continue to be popular throughout the world.

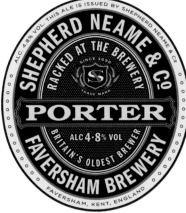

Beau's All Natural

VANKLEEK HILL, CANADA · DESIGN BY JORDAN BAMFORTH

Father and son Tim and Steve Beauchesne opened their Beau's All Natural Brewing Company in 2006. After becoming certified organic, it was clear that shiny, well-polished packaging would not be a fit for this brand. Their rough, environmentally friendly packaging gives their product an honest and approachable feel. Further-ing Beau's DIY ethos, all design work is done in-house by designer Jordan Bamforth.

Their flagship Lug-Tread Lagered Ale is fermented like an ale and then stored cold like a lager, creating a unique brew. This beer is a tribute to a full day's work, drawing its name from tractor tire tracks left in the mud.

Vintage beer labels from the United Kingdom

Brown's Brewing Co. • *Troy, New York, USA* • *Design by id29*

Sauganash Brewing Co.

CHICAGO, ILLINOIS, USA • DESIGN BY JACK MULDOWNEY

This Chicago beer maker draws inspiration from the city's rich history for their small-batch brews. The names of each beer references an early event important to the Chicago's history.

Billy Caldwell, known as Sauganash ("one who speaks English"), was a fur trader born to an Irish father and Mohawk mother. He spoke several languages, leading to his serving as a translator and negotiator among tribes, as well as between Native Americans and the United States government. After negotiating several treaties, the US gave him 1,600 acres along the Chicago River. Part of this land is now the Sauganash neighborhood of Chicago. In 1833, Caldwell helped negotiate the Treaty of Chicago, which led to the removal of American Indians from the area.

Chicago's first hotel opened in 1831 and was also given the Sauganash name. It was strategically located at Wolf Point, the confluence of the North, South, and Main Branches of the Chicago River.

No regional history would be complete without its infamous fire, the state's most famous resident and of course, a splash of corruption. The Sauganash Rye PA

comes much too late to extinguish the flames of the Great Chicago Fire, which famously burned from October 8-10, 1871. The blaze claimed 300 lives and left over 100,000 residents homeless.

In 1864, while riding his horse to the Soldiers' Home, a rifle shot knocked Abraham Lincoln's hat off of his head. The president certainly did not pause to reclaim the topper. This *lost hat*, with a bullet hole in the brim, is now a much sought after piece of memorabilia.

Beer Facts: Abraham Lincoln is in the Wrestling Hall of Fame.

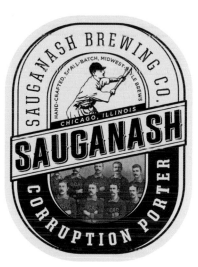

Birth of the Beer Cap

Born in Ireland, mechanical engineer William Painter immigrated to the United States at the age of twenty. He found work as a foreman at the Murrill & Keizer's machine shop in Baltimore. There, Painter helped establish a uniform neck for all glass bottles. This experience led him to create an alternative to the cork stoppers being used (and reused).

In 1892, Painter invented the "crown cork" and opened the Crown Cork & Seal Company. This bottlecap was an immediate success, was cheaper than corks, and provided a better seal. The company currently operates as Crown Holdings, Inc.

William Painter was a prolific inventor. He held 85 patents, which included the bottle opener, a bottle crowning machine, a paper-folding

machine, a safety ejection seat for passenger trains, and a counterfeit coin detector. In 2006, he was inducted to the Inventor Hall of Fame. He also provided the inspiration for another notable invention.

King C. Gillette, a salesman at Crown Cork & Seal, greatly admired the solution that the crown cap provided. A disposable product like this generated its own business. Painter advised Gillette to "Invent something that will be used once and then thrown away. Then the customer will come back for more."

Gillette noted the amount of time men were spending sharpening their shaving blades and saw potential. He would go on to start the wildly successful Gillette Safety Razor Company in 1901.

Coasters Created

Coasters, or "beer mats," developed out of a need to keep bugs and other debris out of beer glasses. The wealthy imbibers had lidded mugs, but the working class needed an inexpensive fix. Early coasters were circular pieces of felt or cardboard, both of which became awfully undesirable after soaking up their share of spilled beer.

In 1892, Robert Sputh of Dresden, Germany, created a more durable option, patenting the wood pulp version that is still popular today. Breweries quickly recognized the advertising opportunity and began printing coasters with logos and advertising slogans.

German bartenders found an additional use for this surface. They would keep patrons' tabs on the beer mats, using different marks to distinguish between drinks types.

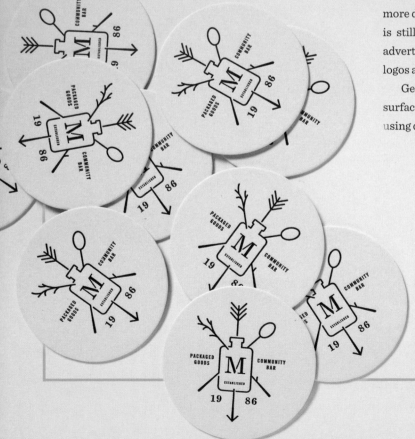

A VERY FINE ALE COMPANY

LOVELAND ALEWORKS

BREWING WITH LOVE IN COLORADO

FILLED WITH MINGLED CREAM AND AMBER
I WILL DRAIN THAT GLASS AGAIN.
SUCH HILARIOUS VISIONS CLAMBER
THROUGH THE CHAMBERS OF MY BRAIN
QUAINTEST THOUGHTS – QUEEREST FANCIES
COME TO LIFE AND FADE AWAY;
WHAT CARE I HOW TIME ADVANCES?
I AM DRINKING ALE TODAY.

EDGAR ALLAN POE

January 17
1920

Prohibition Begins

In 1920 the American temperance movement celebrated victory with the ratification of the 18th Amendment to the Constitution. It was now illegal to manufacture, transport, or sell alcohol—a ban that would last until 1933. During this dry spell, breweries had to get creative to stay in business. They turned their resources to the production of ice cream, malt extract, cheese, soda and near beer. Many just kept quietly brewing beer, slyly distributing it to their customers.

Of course, the United States is not the only country to experience prohibition. The first known instance was when Yu the Great, first ruler of the Chinese Xia Dynasty (2070 BC–1600 BC), banned alcohol throughout the kingdom. Prior to the United States, the early 1900s saw eras of prohibition in Canada, Australia, the Faroe Islands, Iceland, Norway, Russia, Finland, and Hungary. While alcohol was brought back in 1935, standard-strength beer remained illegal in Iceland until 1989. Meanwhile, Prohibition marked a unique era in the United States and launched an iconic and subversive subculture around illegal drinking.

Speakeasy Ales & Lagers

SAN FRANCISCO, CA, USA • DESIGN BY EMRICH OFFICE

During Prohibition, underground bars, or "speakeasies," quickly began popping up, often with direct ties to organized crime. These clubs became social and cultural centers as they filled with men, women, blacks, and whites who refused to abstain from alcohol and a raucous time.

The visual brand of San Francisco's Speakeasy Ales & Lagers captures the spirit of this remarkable time in America's history. Their packaging centers around the central characters of the speakeasy scene, including crime bosses, flappers, jazz singers, and the police.

Our Brewing Company

HOLLAND, MI, USA • DESIGN BY BLINDTIGER DESIGN

The branding for Our Brewing Company harkens back to the pre Prohibition days when each neighborhood had a bar and each neighborhood bar had a friendly (and probably mustachioed bartender) ready to serve.

The design firm at work here also has its roots in this era. During Prohibition, speakeasies were often referred to as "blind tigers." Customers would frequent these establishments and pay a fee to see the blind tiger in the back room. A complimentary beverage was served with the "viewing."

Ken Sakurai (2015)

Landland (2013)

Studio MPLS (2012)

Beer Flows Again

On April 7, 1933, the ban on beer in the United States was finally lifted. Every year, Summit Brewing Co. celebrates a legendary day in American history. The Summit Prohibition Repeal Day posters are designed by a different local designer, screen printed, signed, and numbered.

Aesthetic Apparatus (2009)

April 7
1933

21st Amendment

SAN FRANCISCO, CALIFORNIA, USA • DESIGN BY TBD

The thirteen-year booze drought was fully brought to an end on December 5, 1933, with the ratification of the 21st Amendment. Some states maintained the ban through state temperance laws. The last, Mississippi, stayed dry until 1966.

Sadly, roughly half of the breweries in the United States did not survive to see the end of Prohibition. Just 331 opened their doors in 1933. Thirty years earlier, that number approached 2,000. Many died a slower death as this count slipped into double digits in the 1970s. A new post-Prohibition craft brewery would not open until Jack McAuliffe's short-lived New Albion Brewing launched in 1976.

This period marked a change in beer labels. Before 1920,

labels were simple. They had few colors, few words and uncomplicated graphics. Historically, the amount of text on labels was kept low, often only consisting of the brewery name and city. This was in response to the high illiteracy rate of the beer-drinking demographic. Brewers would also look to fool uneducated consumers by plastering the name of a sexier city across the bottle to make it more appealing.

Prior to Prohibition, breweries and bars served as the living room of their neighborhood. As many of these meeting places disappeared, people began doing more of their drinking at home. Several new packaging methods would debut in the 1930s, at least one of which was being fine tuned throughout the previous decade.

3 | Beer Cans Debut

Anticipating Prohibition's demise, the American Can Company was at work developing the first beer can. There were two main hurdles in this process. The can needed to be strong enough to handle stacking as well as the pressure of carbonated beer. Also, the inside of the can needed a safe lining that would preserve the beer's flavor.

By 1931, American Can Co. finally had a can that was ready to hit shelves. Large brewers Pabst and Anheuser-Busch were both interested in the product. However, fearing consumer reaction, neither wanted to be first. Thus, history was made by Krueger Brewing Co. of Richmond, Virginia. On January 24, 1935, tin cans of their Krueger Cream Ale hit shelves. They were incredible popular with the public, and Krueger's sales increased 550%.

That was enough evidence for Pabst, who became the first major brewer to can their beer in August of 1935. Still a bit hesitant, their first canned beer was labeled Pabst Export, rather using than their prized Blue Ribbon name. By the year's end, twenty-three breweries were canning and more than 200 million beer cans had been sold. Less than a year after Krueger's cans debuted, Welsh brewery Felinfoel became the first European company to offer cans.

Felinfoel adopted the conetop can, which did not require additional machinery. This style, pioneered by Schlitz, was sealed with a crown cap using already existing bottling lines. Flat top cans did not appear in England until the 1950s. Globally, consumer canned beer went on hiatus during World War II as the materials were prioritized for the war effort. Soldiers, however, received canned beer, leading to a burst of popularity when they returned home. Opening instructions would no longer be necessary on can labels. Demand continued and canned beer would outsell bottles for the first time in the United States in 1969.

In 1958, Hawaii's Primo Brewing became the first to switch from tin to aluminum cans. This material would stick, but opening techniques would go through many iterations. Each version either created a sharp piece of metal to be discarded or required the consumer to push a tab through a sharp hole in the can top. This process was finally sorted out with the invention of the "Sta-Tab" in 1975. The beer can would be largely unchanged until wide-mouth openings first appeared in 1997.

Churchkey

SEATTLE, WASHINGTON, USA • DESIGN BY JUSTIN HAWKINS

Can technology has evolved rapidly since its inception, with many types becoming extinct along the way. However, two men are on a quest to resurrect one of them.

As a child, actor Adrian Grenier only knew the churchkey in his grandmother's drawer as a means to open a Hershey's syrup can. The flat-top can was the standard from 1935 until the 1960s, but disappeared with the invention of the pull tab can. Decades later, he met former Nike designer Justin Hawkins and the two vowed to bring back the flat-top can. The vintage beer packaging, designed by Hawkins, includes a churchkey opener and an overall experience new to most of us.

1936

Steinies & Stubbies

Beginning in the 1930s, the popularity of canned beer soared. One group of people, however, was less than thrilled about this new packaging style—the glass industry. The large number of breweries beginning to can their beer became a major threat to a very large market for glassmakers. So in response, they invented two new bottle shapes, the stubby and the steinie. Both styles were much shorter (similar in height to a can) and stocky. They also stacked more efficiently like cans. The steinie has a bulging tapered neck, modeled after the taller export bottles. These were created by the Owens-Illinois Glass Company in 1936. The stubby style has an exaggeratedly small neck and typically hold eleven or twelve ounces.

Each bottle style enjoyed a run of success in the United States. Major brands such as Schlitz and Budweiser were filling steinies with their product. The use of steinies fell off by the 1950s as stubbies became more popular. Today, the 375 milliliter steinie is widely available throughout Europe, particularly with Belgian beers (such as Daas). Stubbies were used almost exclusively in Canada from 1961 until 1984 before disappearing again from the market. Today this style can still be commonly found in Australia and New Zealand. Several American brands, including Coors, have reintroduced this style to embrace the nostalgia for the bottle.

Kagua • Tokyo, Japan • Design by Mitsuyoshi Miyazaki

Full Sail Brewing Co.

HOOD RIVER, OREGON, USA • DESIGN BY SANDSTROM PARTNERS

When Full Sail first brewed their Session Premium Lager, they brought back a pre-Prohibition style beer that was approachable and unpretentious. A no-nonsense bottle from that era was the perfect fit for this classic lager. In 2005 the beer hit shelves in 11oz stubby bottles. That year, it went on to become the fastest growing brand in American craft beer.

The bold, restrained design and diamond bounding shape would fit right into the 1940s market. These bottles made older consumers reminiscent of the Olympia stubbies that once blanketed the Pacific Northwest.

Be careful not to write this beer off as a packaging novelty. This beer has filled a trophy case with awards, including winning gold at GABF and being named "World's Best Premium Lager" at the World Beer Awards.

Nijenrode Bier

BREUKELEN, NETHERLANDS • DESIGN BY POSITIVITY

This Dutch brewery draws its name from the nearby castle. "Nijenrode" means "newly developed ground," which is appropriate as design firm Positivity recently broke ground on a redesign.

They retained the coat of arms and the steinie bottle shape and tore everything else down. The resulting label is classy, but not snobby, and immediately recognizable. Stripping away the paper label allows the Burgues Script typeface from Sudtipos to take center stage. The use of only one color throughout the label immediately establishes an identifiable brand color. Yellow, incidentally, is the primary color of the Breukelen coat of arms.

Unsurprisingly, Nijenrode has become a big hit with students from the neighboring university of the same name, which also utilizes the town's coat of arms in its logo.

North Peak Brewing Co. • Traverse City, Michigan, USA • Design by Neatly Trimmed Beard & Irene Tomoko Sugiura

Six-Packs Hit the Shelf

The six-pack was one of several new beer packages introduced in the 1930s. Drinking at home was suddenly much more popular and breweries wanted to make it as easy as possible for consumers to do just that. Various breweries are credited as the first to package their offerings in six, but it seems as though we can agree that they debuted in 1938. Research studies at the time decided that six beers was the optimal weight for housewives to carry home from the store.

The trendsetter here was actually Coca-Cola, who in 1923 began selling bottles of their product in boxes of six.

Good People Brewing Co. • Birmingham, Alabama, USA • Design by Lewis Communication

Hopper Whitman • *Novato, California, USA* • *Design by Stranger & Stranger*

Walker Brown • Novato, California, USA • Design by Stranger & Stranger

4 | The Craft Beer Movement

Many American breweries were not able to weather the storm that was Prohibition. There were nearly 2,000 breweries at the turn of the century. However, when Prohibition was lifted in 1933, only 331 were still standing. This number reached a low in 1978 when just 89 breweries were in operation. Fewer breweries meant larger market shares and the strong got stronger. "Big Beer" was king. Eventually, small breweries would rise again.

In 1965, a young Stanford graduate learned that the makers of his favorite beer, were planning on closing their doors. Fritz Maytag visited Anchor Brewing the next day and soon put together a few thousand dollars to purchase 51% of the company and save it from bankruptcy. In three years he would own the remaining shares. The total price, as he puts it, was "less than the price of a used car."

This new era of Anchor would be marked by cautious growth and an emphasis on quality. It took time to raise the brewery from the edge of financial disaster, but Anchor beer became a huge regional success, eventually breaking out as the pioneer of a new era of American beer. Maytag's hands-on, detail-driven approach went on to be represented visually by the beautifully hand-drawn labels that would adorn each Anchor beer.

Anchor Brewing Co.

SAN FRANCISCO, CALIFORNIA, USA • DESIGN BY JIM STITT

The history of Anchor Brewing begins long before Fritz Maytag, at the California Gold Rush of 1849. Many of these fortune-seekers were Europeans who brought their thirst for lagers. California was too warm for the traditional lager brewing process, so brewers had to get creative. Without ice to cool the wort, beer was placed in large, shallow, open pans on the rooftops of the breweries. As the beer cooled, clouds of steam lifted from the buildings and gave name to a new beer style. By 1900 there were over a hundred steam breweries in California. Anchor, however, was the only one left standing after Prohibition lifted in 1933.

Wary of lesser-quality beers ruining their reputation, Fritz trademarked "steam beer" in 1981. Similar style beers are now classified as "California common beers."

Steam was not the only popular beer style during the Gold Rush as English IPAs quickly gained a following. The design of Anchor's IPA label is a nod to the Allsop label that was arriving in California. The elephant, however, comes from a popular expression of the day. Forty-niners headed west to "see the elephant" and the animal became a symbol for this exotic adventure. Elephant sketches appeared in many of their travel journals. The main character on the Anchor IPA label is heading west, symbolizing the beer's journey from England to California.

An English-style ale was added to the Anchor lineup in 1975. With America's upcoming bicentennial, they named it Liberty Ale and prominently featured an eagle on the label. The lettering is inspired by the work of 18th century typographer John Baskerville.

> *I try to avoid computerish-looking work. It's a handmade beer, so the label should be hand-drawn.*
> —Jim Stitt

Local artist Jim Stitt is responsible for almost every Anchor beer label since the 1970s. Once a technical illustrator for Boeing, Stitt now works from his boat in Sausalito. His skilled hand gives each Anchor label a historical, handmade quality, beginning with the Anchor Porter label in 1974.

Every year since 1975, Anchor has brewed their Christmas Ale with a unique recipe. And each year, they have called upon Stitt to create a unique label to accompany the brew. The label for their 39th Christmas Ale (right) features the California White Fir.

Some years the tree on the label is simply one that caught the eye of Maytag during the year. Other times there is special meaning behind the choice. When Maytag got married in 1987, Stitt symbolically used two trees, a Douglas fir and a redwood, for that year's label.

While nearly 100,000 rushed to California in search of gold, Cornish plant collector William Lobb arrived in 1849 looking for trees. Employed by the Veitch Nurseries of Exeter, England, Lobb collected the seeds of fifty-eight species of California plants to be first introduced to England. These findings including the Giant Sequoia, California Juniper and California White Fir.

1975: The Original Christmas Ale Tree.

1976: Giant Sequoia

1980: Oak Tree

1983: Greek Fir

1987: Douglas Fir & Coast Redwood

1995: Coconut Palm

2004: Inspired by the Original Tree.

2009: Monterey Cypress

2012: Norfolk Island Pine

Homebrewing Returns

Beer has been brewed in homes for thousands of years. The role of the brewer has always been an important one, frequently carried out by women throughout history. Ancient recipes were often preserved on tablets, as well as through songs and prayers due to high illiteracy rates. In the United States, this rich history came to an end in 1920.

Prohibition shut down every brewery in the United States, also putting an end to homebrewing, a practice which would remain illegal for almost sixty years. This ban was finally lifted on October 14, 1978, when President Jimmy Carter signed H.R. 1337 into law. Before the year was up, Charlie Papazian and Charlie Matzen had founded the American Homebrewers Association. In 1978 there were only 89 breweries in the country. The passing of this bill would launch future craft brewers across thousands of kitchens in the United States. By 2014 there were 3,464 breweries on American soil.

In 1984, nuclear engineer Charlie Papazian published *The Complete Joy of Homebrewing*. Over a million copies of the book have since been sold, guiding new homebrewers through their exciting new hobby. Now in its fourth edition, this landmark book is often referred to as "the homebrewer's bible."

On July 1, 2013, homebrewing finally became legal across the United States as homebrewing legislation passed in Mississippi. Measures in other countries have opened the door for a homebrewing revival as well. In 1963 the United Kingdom no longer required homebrewers purchase a license. Just weeks after taking office, Australian Prime Minister Gough Whitlam legalized the practice in 1972.

American Homebrewers Association email campaign photo by Luke Trautwein.

Sierra Nevada

CHICO, CALIFORNIA, USA • DESIGN BY AUSTON DESIGN GROUP

When founder Ken Grossman first visited Chico, California, he instantly fell in love. He moved in and opened a homebrew store downtown. As time went on, his homebrewing escalated and in 1980 Grossman opened a small scale brewery. He named his new venture after the nearby mountain range that he frequently hiked.

Sierra Nevada's flagship Pale Ale proudly stars the Cascade hop, as does the beer's label. The release of this hop in 1971 played an important role in the craft brewing revolution. It was developed in Oregon and proved that a quality hop could be grown outside of Europe. The Cascade hop was embraced by West Coast brewers and became a star ingredient of the craft beer emergence.

To celebrate the brewery's 30th anniversary, Ken Grossman decided to pay tribute to the men who ushered in the craft beer awakening. He brought in Fritz Maytag (Anchor Brewing), Jack McAuliffe (New Albion Brewery) and beer advocates Fred Eckhardt and Charlie Papazian. Four collaboration beers were brewed in honor of these men "who launched a thousand breweries."

LIFE and LIMB

LIFE – this living ale is naturally carbonated to enhance complexity, refinement, and to encourage aging. LIMB – for the birch and maple trees, whose syrup gives this ale its unique flavor and symbolizes the collaboration between Sierra Nevada and Dogfish Head. We are proud to share our Life and Limb with the thousands of other branches who collectively comprise the craft-brewing family tree. Sip slowly with friends and loved ones; savor—because one could do better than be a swigger of birches.

24 FL. OZ.

www.Life-Limb.com

ALE WITH MAPLE SYRUP & BIRCH SYRUP ADDED
1 PT 8 FL OZ CA REDEMPTION VALUE

Sierra Nevada / Dogfish Head Brewery "Life and Limb"

CHICO, CALIFORNIA, USA • MILTON, DELAWARE, USA •
DESIGN BY JEREMY HOLMES

Much like Jim Stitt, Jeremy Holmes carefully hand-crafts his beer labels. For the fairy tale "Life and Limb" collaboration between Sierra Nevada and Dogfish Head, brewery founders Ken Grossman and Sam Calagione turned to this award-winning children's book illustrator. The result is a highly rated beer with a very unique and intricate label.

This American Strong Ale is built upon maple syrup from the Calagione family farm in Massachusetts and barley grown at the Sierra Nevada brewery in California, and is naturally carbonated with Alaskan birch syrup. The yeast used is a blend of the two breweries' house strains. All of this combines for a very complex and earthy beer.

The same can be said for the beer's label. You will notice the two tree trunks merging together to symbolize the breweries, the prominent syrup tap and plenty of small details in the tree and background which reference Sam, Ken and their breweries.

Both the California state bird (Valley Quail) and the Delaware state bird (Blue Hen) make an appearance. In the tree you will find a bicycle sprocket for Ken's riding hobby and a guitar referencing Calagione's beer geek hip-hop group, the Pain Relievaz.

Samuel Adams

BOSTON, MA, USA · DESIGN BY THE BOSTON BEER COMPANY

Meanwhile, on the East Coast, the craft beer revolution began with ties to a rebellion of another kind. After graduating from Harvard University in 1743, founding father Samuel Adams was unsure about his future. He decided to join the family business and became a partner in his family's malt house that had been passed down through several generations. Soon enough he would abandon his role in the beer industry for his true calling in politics, eventually becoming a leader of the American Revolution.

Many years later, Jim Koch also graduated from Harvard with questions about his future. After a brief stint in business consulting, he too turned to the family business. His father was a fifth-generation brewer and passed down the recipes from Louis Koch. Louis, Jim's great-great-grandfather, emigrated from Germany and opened a brewery in St. Louis. The Louis Koch brewery did not survive Prohibition, but would find a second life with Jim.

Jim Koch began brewing Samuel Adams Boston Lager in his kitchen. He filled his old briefcase with bottles of the brew and took to the streets selling it to local bars and restaurants. The beer officially launched in 1985 and was carried in 25 venues. Six weeks later it would be named "The Best Beer in America" at the Great American Beer Festival.

The instincts of this revolutionary thinker were correct. His brewery vaulted to success and is now produces more than two million barrels annually.

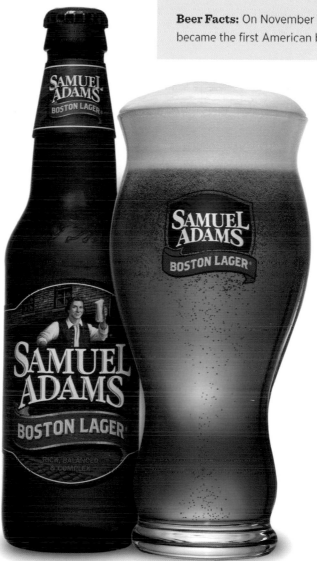

Beer Facts: On November 13, 1985, Boston Lager became the first American beer sold in Germany.

Brooklyn Brewery

BROOKLYN, NEW YORK, USA • DESIGN BY MILTON GLASER

When Steve Hindy and Tom Potter were creating Brooklyn Eagle Beer (as it was going to be called) they interviewed dozens of design firms. All along, the guy at the very top of their list was Milton Glaser. After calling every day for two weeks, Milton's secretary finally let Steve talk to the designer. Steve told Milton that he was looking for a logo that every guy in Brooklyn would want tattooed. Glaser quickly talked the pair into a name change. "Call it Brooklyn! Why do you want to be represented by a bird, when you can own the whole borough?" The now-legendary logo followed soon thereafter.

Founder Steve Hindy with Milton Glaser

Growlers Grow Up

In 1989, Charlie and Ernie Otto found themselves in need of a solution. After founding the first modern microbrewery in Wyoming, they wanted to find a way to offer to-go beer to their customers. However, their year-old Otto Brothers' Brewing Company was not yet ready to make the financial jump into bottling. The brothers found their answer in a product that technology had long left behind.

Upon hearing about the predicament, their father told them about the "growler" that patrons once used to carry fresh beer home from the bar. Recognizing that the tin pail was no longer practical, the brothers set out to modernize the concept. Charlie purchased the necessary equipment and began silkscreening the brewery logo onto sixty-four ounce refillable cider jugs. Thus, the modern growler was born. After three years of legislation, the brothers

succeeded in making the brew pub legal in the state of Wyoming and were able to sell their growlers directly to customers.

Success dictated a need for a larger space and Otto Brothers opened up a larger brewery at the base of Teton Pass in Victor, Idaho. They embraced their new locale changing the company name to Grand Teton Brewing in 2000. In 2009 Steve and Ellen Furbacher purchased the brewery.

Obviously since 1989 countless breweries have offered growlers poured directly from their taps. It has become a staple of the brewpub and no oddity in gas stations. Since its advent the growler can be found in many more shapes, sizes and materials as companies continue to try to advance that original lidded pail. Filling and sanitizing techniques have also become a focus area for improvement.

The current Grand Teton growlers

Rogue Ales
Newport, Oregon, USA
Design by Penny Muire

Holy Mountain Brewing Co.
Seattle, Washington, USA
Design by Adam Paysse

Top Hops
New York, New York, USA
Design by Helms Workshop

Dru Bru • Snoqualmie Pass, Washington, USA • Design by Scott V. Fuller

Steel & Oak Brewing • New Westminster, Canada • Design by Also Known As: Design Studio

Shine Craft Vessels • Richmond, Virginia, USA • Design by Jordan Childs

DEDICATED TO THE CRAFT

BALLAST POINT
BREWING COMPANY

SCULPIN
INDIA PALE ALE

A TROPHY BEER
THAT'S A TESTAMENT
OUR HOMEBREW ROOTS

Our Sculpin IPA is a great
example of what got us
into brewing in the first place.
After years of experimenting,
we knew hopping an ale in
five separate stages would
produce something special.
The result ended up being
this gold medal-winning IPA,
whose inspired use of hops
creates hints of apricot,
peach, mango and lemon
flavors, but still packs
a sting. Just like a Sculpin.

DEDICATED TO THE CRAFT
BALLASTPOINT.COM
10051 Old Grove Road
San Diego, CA 92131

5 | A Can Comeback

For decades, consumers maintained hardened opinions about the difference between bottles and cans. Anything in a can was cheap, light and meant to be chugged at a temperature cold enough to avoid tasting its cheapness. A beer of any merit came in a bottle. Simple.

Recently, that perception has been reexamined. As craft beer marched in, consumers made careful decisions about what they drank, as well as what they drank out of.

This new and more aware beer drinker favors buying cans for a number of reasons. Beer cans stack more efficiently than bottles, thus leaving a smaller footprint during the shipping process. They also recycle at a much higher rate than bottles. Canned beer is completely shielded from light, which causes beer to become "skunked." Gone are the days where you needed to worry about canned beer tasting metallic (thanks science!). With cans, drinking in the great outdoors becomes glass shard-free. For designers, cans offer a larger, continuous canvas, leading to fresh ideas.

Oskar Blues

LONGMONT, COLORADO, USA • DESIGN BY TERRY KISHIYAMA

In 2002 Oskar Blues took a big, bold step, becoming the first American craft brewery to can their beers in-house. At just five years old, this was a major gamble for the brewery. Craft contract brewer Chief Oshkosh began canning their red lager in 1991, but the timing proved to be poor, and the brewery closed in 1994.

Consumers' perceptions about canned beer was just one hurdle for Oskar Blues to overcome. Another issue was equipment. Into the 1990s, cans and canning lines were only being produced for huge breweries. Thus, machinery and minimum can orders were both very large and prohibitively expensive for a small brewery. During this decade there was a microbrewery explosion that proved to be more than the market could bear. After many quickly closed their doors, the stage was set for Oskar Blues.

After many of their customers disappeared, Canadian equipment provider Cask Brewing Systems got creative. They created a small, affordable hand-canning line and convinced Ball Corporation to drastically reduce their minimum order requirement. In 2002 they convinced Oskar Blues to pioneer the system. They released Dale's Pale Ale in cans and have never looked back. Two years later they expanded their canning operation by 400%. In 2005, *The New York Times* declared their flagship beer the best pale ale in the country. The following year they broke through as the largest brewpub in the United States.

21st Amendment

SAN FRANCISCO, CALIFORNIA, USA • DESIGN BY TBD •

ILLUSTRATIONS BY JON CONTINO

With hop prices skyrocketing during the hop crisis of 2008, breweries quickly began cutting back on their usage. Instead of following suit, 21st Amendment went all in with this extremely hoppy Imperial IPA weighing in at 9.7% ABV. Columbus, Centennial, and Cascade hops are used for bittering in this beer, which is dry-hopped with Simcoe, Ahtanum, Amarillo, and Cascade and aged on oak.

The packaging tells the story of brothers Shaun and Nico, who must break out of Alcatraz. They plan a daring escape to free the hops from the Hop Syndicate, who is hoarding them in a remote warehouse.

This packaging was created as 21st Amendment found themselves battling against consumers who did not believe high-end beer could come in cans. They conducted research which showed that consumers of premium beers were heavily engaged in the story of a beer. Thus, 21st Amendment began writing elaborate tales for each of their varieties.

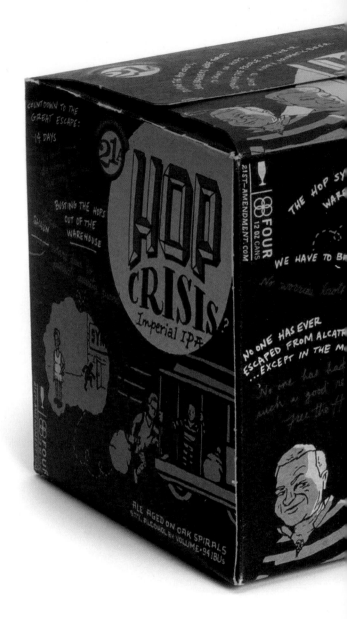

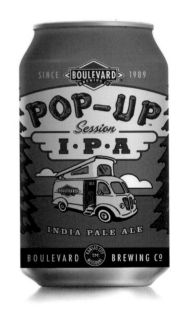

Boulevard Brewing Co. • *Kansas City, Missouri, USA* • *Design by Boulevard Brewing*

Hops & Grain Brewery • Austin, Texas, USA • Design by Derouen & Co.

Tin Man Brewing Co.

EVANSVILLE, INDIANA, USA • DESIGN BY MATT WAGNER DESIGN

This brewery name is not a *Wizard of Oz* reference, but rather a nod to founder Nick Davidson's childhood robot obsession. After a decade of homebrewing, Davidson made the jump and moved into a building that has been a furniture store, boarding house, liquor store, and swap meet in previous lives. The original wood floor was pulled up and repurposed as tabletops. Brewery visitors are greeted by a 300 pound, 6'7" metal mascot.

Tin Man's first releases are all sessionable beers, served on nitrogen at the brewery. Rivet (5.1% ABV) has become the favorite in the taproom. This well-balanced Irish Red is brewed with caramel malts and packs plenty of sweet toffee and dark fruit flavors.

Bold City Brewery • Jacksonville, Florida, USA • Design by Kendrick Kidd

Sixpoint Brewery

NEW YORK, NEW YORK, USA • DESIGN BY LEFTY LEXINGTON

Sixpoint opened up in Red Hook, Brooklyn, a neighborhood full of maritime history. Many of their neighboring warehouses display the five-pointed nautical star. Following their lead, Sixpoint's logo blends this star with the historic brewer's star.

Brewers have been marking their barrels and buildings with six-pointed stars for at least 1,300 years. The points represent grain, water, hops, yeast, malt, and the brewer. During the 1500s, it became the official mark of the Brewer's Guild. According to the brewery's tagline, "The Sixpoint star navigates you to good beer."

Sixpoint has rebuffed typical beer styles, rolling out their "concept beers." Their cans do not list a beer style—just ounces, IBUs, ABV, color, and an atypical description. For example:

Ah love is bitter and sweet,
but which is more sweet
the bitterness or the sweetness,
none has spoken it.

Bauhaus Brew Labs

MINNEAPOLIS, MINNESOTA, USA • DESIGN BY HELMS WORKSHOP

"Play becomes celebration; celebration becomes work; work becomes play," wrote Johannes Itten, teacher at the influential Bauhaus school. This early 20th century German design school sought to unify art, craft, and technology while injecting a playfulness and thirst for exploration. Its founders observed a growing and unnecessary separation between art and manufacturing. Their short-lived, yet wildly influential guild bridged this gap for future canned beer art.

Believing in a balance between seriousness and fun,

they are well known for both their groundbreaking design work as well as their boisterous parties.

Bauhaus Brew Labs extends its namesake's spirit into the beer-making world. These musicians, scientists, and artists combine to create German-style beers. Their brightly colored cans add an element of fun to their thoughtfully crafted beers. Each style's peculiar name is the product of translating conventional names into German and then back into English.

The Alchemist

WATERBURY, VERMONT, USA • DESIGN BY DAN BLAKESLEE

The Alchemist realized there was money to be made packaging their beer after discovering a pub customer had beat them to it. A patron was bringing full pints into the restroom, pouring them into bottles, and affixing a home-made label he made using images from their website.

They found the artist for their cans at the Muddy Waters Cafe in Burlington, Vermont. While frequenting the establishment, owner John Kimmich spotted Dan Blakesee drawing a poster for an upcoming concert. He soon began illustrating coasters, shirts, and the famous Heady Topper cans. For these, Kimmich wanted a character whose head was exploding with hops. The end result was one who inadvertently looks much like the artist (minus the exploding head).

It would be impossible to overstate the frenzy around this world-class double IPA. They produce 2.5 million cans

annually, only distributing within a twenty-mile radius of the brewery. Thirsty adventurers travel from all over the country to get their hands on it and each can sells out within a few hours of hitting the shelf. Black market sales of the beer have become a big enough problem that the Vermont Department of Liquor Control has set up stings to slow down trafficking of Heady Topper, which is currently the highest rated beer on BeerAdvocate.

While other craft brewers are creating specialized glassware to better present their beers, The Alchemist insists that this one is enjoyed directly from the can. "Drink it from the can." is boldly printed at the top of each container. On March 21, 2015, The Alchemist added a second can to their lineup, Focal Banger IPA. This beer quickly received world-class rankings, with many drinkers boldy claiming it has overtaken Heady Topper as the top IPA. Taking a different approach than Heady Topper's mysterious blend of six hops, Focal Banger is crafted with Mosaic and Citra hops from Oregon and weighs in at a slightly lower 7% ABV.

Modern Times

SAN DIEGO, CALIFORNIA, USA • DESIGN BY HELMS WORKSHOP • LOGOTYPE BY SIMON WALKER

Modern Times was a utopian community built on Long Island in 1850 by "a bunch of wild-eyed wingnuts" looking to demonstrate a more perfect society. Appreciating their quirky ambition, founder Jacob McKean named his Southern California brewery in their honor.

Their beers are also named after real and fabled utopian projects, including Blazing World Amber, Fortunate Islands Wheat, Black House Stout, and Lomaland Saison.

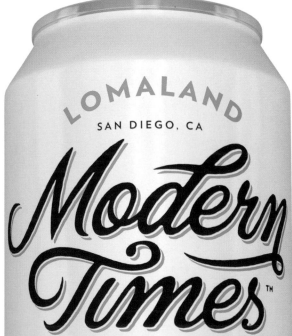

Defiance Brewing Co.

HAYS, KANSAS, USA • DESIGN BY JOHN STADLER

The Defiance brand stands for, among other things, breaking away from mass-produced beer. They wrap their "ambitious beer" in adventurous artwork overflowing with illustrated personality. The design for their first release, Thrasher Session IPA, pays homage to their small-town beginnings. As the can implies, there is something big brewing in Hays, Kansas.

The Gutch can sets a social scene where English and American characters mix. In this English-style beer, ingredients and brewing techniques from the two nations merrily mingle as well.

Steamworks Brewing

VANCOUVER, CANADA • DESIGN BY BRANDEVER

In 1867, steamboat captain "Gassy" Jack Deighton settled in Vancouver and opened the first bar in the area. When Steamworks Brewing first entered their building in this historic neighborhood, now known as "Gastown," they discovered a rather unusual feature. It was equipped with a rare steam heating system, which they fully embraced, becoming Canada's first steam-powered brewery.

Brandever was able to create a brand that ties together the brewery's historic home and the important role of steam in the operation. Their playful illustrations create steampunk versions of some of Vancouver's most notable architecture.

Daredevil Brewing Co.

SPEEDWAY, INDIANA, USA • DESIGN BY CULTIVATOR ADVERTISING & DESIGN

This Indiana brewery is not afraid to take a risk, nor is it afraid to go a little further to get what it wants. After falling in love with the name, they discovered a defunct Australian winery still held a trademark for "Daredevil." Rather than settling with another name, they pushed forward. After five months of negotiations they were able to secure it. Their "aggressively fun" concoctions are now available throughout their home state.

Evil Twin Brewing

NEW YORK, NEW YORK, USA • DESIGN BY MARTIN JUSTESEN

Martin Justesen has created an iconic, geometric brand for Denmark's renowned Evil Twin Brewing. Founded in 2010 by Jeppe Jarnit-Bjergsø, this gypsy brewer makes "exquisite craft beers for crispy beer geeks, tasty gourmands, and you." As the brewery name alludes to, Jeppe is the twin brother of Mikkel Borg Bjergsø of Mikkeller.

Hipster Ale was created for wanna-be-hipsters who are unfortunate enough to live in non-hipster neighborhoods. This "hip without border" American Pale Ale was brewed at Two Roads Brewing in Stratford, Connecticut.

Beau's All Natural • Vankleek Hill, Canada • Design by Jordan Bamforth

6 | Modern Design Themes

As craft beer booms, store shelves are getting more and more competitive. With more than 15,000 breweries worldwide, breweries have recognized that it takes more than just remarkable beer to drive sales. They are investing in design as a means to separate themselves. Packaging is often the first way a consumer interacts with a brand, making it a great opportunity to stand out. Many breweries choose to use their labels to personify their craftsmanship and creativity or to tell the story behind their company. Others choose a different route for their visual brand.

As in other markets, certain design themes are emerging in beer packaging design. Minimalism is certainly a clear example of this. Some breweries are straying as far from the "big beer" brands as possible. They are countering with packaging with a handcrafted aesthetic, further contrasting the hands-on approach of their small operation. Others in this vein identify with a hand-drawn, illustrated, or even graffiti look. Counter to this trend, nostalgia of the previous beer eras is being embraced by those opting for a more retro design approach. Time-honored shapes and styles are brought back, recalling a time when the beer scene was very different.

When brewery numbers were at their highest, and distribution was not yet born, consumers were loyal to their town or neighborhood brewery. This sentiment has returned through an overwhelming number of breweries. They are anchoring their brand to local names, geography and historical elements. Some, however, choose a visual identity unique all to their own.

Packaging has also become a means to encroach upon other markets. Beer is no longer just a fizzy yellow reward for the working class. Modern brews exist for every occasion and every demographic. Premium brands are positioning themselves thusly with extravagant packaging solutions previously reserved for wine and champagne. When executed properly, spending extra on elaborate packaging expands a brewery's consumer base and raises their stature.

UNION Craft Brewing • Baltimore, Maryland, USA • Design by Natalie Cone / Gilah Press, Jon Zerivitz

R&B Brewing Co. • *Vancouver, Canada* • *St. Bernadine Mission Communication*

KAIJU!

MELBOURNE, AUSTRALIA • DESIGN BY MIKEY BURTON

After a certain energy drink took umbrage with the "Monster Mash" name, this brewery rebranded. To mark this transformation, Metamorphosis IPA was the first beer released under the new moniker.

"Kaiju" is Japanese for "strange creature," thus the owners found themselves in need of some, well, strange creatures. The supremely talented illustrator Mikey Burton provided them with a cast of characters primed to leap off store shelves.

Mikkeller

COPENHAGEN, DENMARK • DESIGN BY KEITH SHORE

This unusual packaging is for a most unusual Danish brewery. Mikkeller began in 2006 with homebrewers Mikkel Borg Bjergsø and Kristian Klarup Keller, who left the venture in 2007. Mikkel has gone on to produce well over six hundred different beers, whose flavors test the brewing boundaries. Mikkeller has had many beers ranked among the elite by RateBeer and BeerAdvocate.

The brewery's early labels included sketched portraits of Mikkel and Kristian that caught the eye of New Jersey artist Keith Shore. He saw a good fit and emailed the brewery about a possible collaboration. Soon thereafter, Shore created the label for "I Hardcore You" in his signature (and earless) illustration style. Many labels would follow, creating one of the most recognizable brands on the shelf.

440 ml

6% ALC.VOL

Brewed by
Devil's Peak
Company

THE KING'S

HAND-CRAFTED

BLOCKHOUSE
IPA

Devil's Peak Brewing Co. • Cape Town, South Africa • Designed by Just Design

Uinta Brewing
Salt Lake City, Utah, USA
Design by Emrich Office

Beau's All Natural
Vankleek Hill, Canada
Design by Jordan Bamforth

Kona Brewing Co.
Kona, Hawaii, USA
Design by Flint Design Co.

Flying Dog Brewery

FREDERICK, MARYLAND, USA • DESIGN BY RALPH STEADMAN

Hunter S. Thompson moved to Woody Creek, Colorado, in 1969 and soon became close friends with neighbor George Stranahan. The two bonded over common interests in high-powered weapons, politics, football, whiskey, and beer.

In 1983, astrophysicist, photographer, rancher, writer, philanthropist, and educator Stranahan set out to climb the second highest mountain in the world, K2. This mountain has claimed 84 lives and justly earned the nickname "Savage Mountain." The toughest part of the grueling trek though, according to Stranahan, was "on day 17 of a 35-day trip, we totally ran out of booze."

Upon completing the expedition, Stranahan and his crew found themselves celebrating victoriously back at the hotel bar in Pakistan. There, a bizarre oil painting caught their attention. The subject of the painting was a "flying dog"—words that would stick with George for years. As he explains, "They fit together in some way. I don't know how it makes sense, but it makes sense."

In 1990, George Stranahan opened Flying Dog Brewpub in Aspen, Colorado. Four years later they opened their large brewing facility in Frederick, Maryland.

Hunter S. Thompson introduced Stranahan to his longtime illustrator Ralph Steadman, who began creating the artwork for Flying Dog's labels in 1996. His first label was for Road Dog Porter. In addition to his frenetic, in-your-face style art, he also adorned this label with "Good Beer, No Shit." The Colorado State Liquor Board insisted the phrase be banned, but after five years of court battles and assistance from the ACLU, it proudly graces the beer's label once again.

Thompson was not the only fortunate neighbor George Stranahan had during his time in Colorado. Once, when his barn caught on fire, volunteer firefighter Jess Graber responded to his neighbor's blaze. After disaster was averted, the two struck up conversation and discovered a mutual affinity for fine whiskey. They would eventually open Stranahan's Colorado Whiskey.

White Rabbit Brewery • Healesville, Australia • Design by braincells

Microbrasserie du Lac • St-Jean Saint-Gédéon, Quebec, Canada • Design by doiion

Saint Arnold Brewing

HOUSTON, TEXAS, USA • DESIGN BY CARLOS HERNANDEZ

Founded in 1994, Saint Arnold is Texas' oldest craft brewery. Brock Wagner and Kevin Bartol named their company after one of beer's patron saints, Saint Arnold of Metz. This monk was instrumental in ending a plague outbreak by convincing people to drink beer instead of the contaminated water.

In 2011 the brewery released Santo, a screaming change from the rest of the Saint Arnold lineup. The process for this beer was completely backward and resulted in a made-up beer style.

Typically a brewery creates a beer and then turns to the designer for artwork that expresses its various characteristics visually. Santo actually began at a 2008 art show. Brewery founder Brock Wagner attended the opening of local artist Carlos Hernandez's "Day of the Dead Rock Stars." Wagner left the show with a monstrous "El John Lennon" painting (which still hangs in his office) and inspiration for a new project. He later hired Hernandez to create art that the brewery interpreted in beer form. Their most accurate classification for Santo is a black Kölsch, which you certainly are not going to find in your BJCP style guidelines (yet).

Odell Brewing Co.

FORT COLLINS, COLORADO, USA • DESIGN BY TBD

This hand-lettered elm leaf logo is everything you could hope for from a brewery that names its milk stout after the dairy farmer who collects their spent grains. The Odell brand stands for sustainability and craftsmanship. Their bottles are made of 70% recycled material and come from less than 10 miles away. The brewery utilizes solar panels, as well as solar tubes, which maximize natural light inside the brewery during the day.

Design firm TBD visualized the ethos of the brand and crafted a redesign of Odell's main line beers, which helped increase sales by 40%. The labels feature illustrations by Mona Caron and a gorgeous hand-drawn typeface inspired by Cowboy Rhumbahut. This rebranding was successful because, as Director of Sales and Marketing Eric Smith explains, it represents "high quality beer made by real people."

Cerveza Tyris

VALENCIA, SPAIN • DESIGN BY ESTUDIO MLLONGO

When Spanish brewer Tyris decided to make an American pale ale, they went all the way to Dixie for inspiration—and maybe a good-spirited jab. Sprawling, disorderly handwriting and the simple color palette give the Au Yeah! an approachable unsophistication. The beer's banjo-wielding spokesman makes you want to pull up a rocking chair and give this one a try.

Lakewood Brewery / Rahr & Sons "DFW"

DALLAS, TEXAS, USA • DESIGN BY ALL THE PRETTY COLORS

As the label's entangled beards suggest, DFW is a collaboration brew from Dallas-Fort Worth area breweries Lakewood and Rahr & Sons. The two companies strayed a bit from classic Belgian styles to inject flavors from their heritage. Lakewood's owner and brewer Wim Bens is a Belgian native who started his career working for the German-rooted Fritz Rahr. Their Belgian yeast, candi sugar, and German malt blend mesh together in this malty, sweet Belgian-inspired dubbel. The limited-edition, screen-printed bottles debuted during North Texas Beer Week 2014.

Pretty Things Beer & Ale Project

SOMERVILLE, MASSACHUSETTS, USA • DESIGN BY DANN & MARTHA PAQUETTE

Founders Dann and Martha Paquette first met at a Real Ale festival in Somerville, Massachusetts. On their second date, Dann was attracted to a framed piece of embroidery made by Martha's grandmother. He immediately told her the white tree on a red crest would become the logo for their future brewery.

The two married and moved to Martha's native England. There, Dann started working at a local brewery and the two explored nearby towns and pubs. On one such adventure, they came across a cathedral which overlooked an ancient Saxon crypt. Further investigation revealed a surprising source of glee and inspiration. "For us, the jewels of the cathedral are the 15th century misericord carvings in the choir. Pigs play the bagpipes, swimmers are snatched by sea monsters, apes fight lions, and Pliny's mysterious 'Blemya' inhabit this magical world. These carvings struck a chord with us because they are vivid, ancient, insanely full of personality, and fun. Fun is an important word to us."

Dann continued his brewing career when the couple moved back to Massachusetts and the two eventually opened Pretty Things Beer & Ale Project. They are tenant brewers, currently producing their beers at Buzzards Bay Brewing in Westport, MA. Dann and Martha form the recipes, brew the beer, and draw the labels which are inspired by those whimsical creatures carved into the Yorkshire cathedral.

The Pretty Things Beer & Ale Project gets its name from a favorite band of Dann Paquette. The Pretty Things are an English rock band who originally lifted the name from the Bo Diddley's song "Pretty Thing."

Popular in the 1960s, The Pretty Things enjoyed success in the UK, Australia and New Zealand. They would later be banned from New Zealand after drummer Viv Prince set a bag of crayfish on fire mid-flight. Apparently, the cathedral's wood carvings were not the only whimsical characters to inspire the brand of this brewery.

Feral Brewing Co.

PERTH, AUSTRALIA • DESIGN BY BLOCK BRANDING

Feral Brewing Company is Western Australia's largest independent brewery, operating smack dab in its oldest wine region. When it came time to redesign, Feral sought a stark contrast with not only the area's wine brands, but also all of the other beer brands on the shelf. They identified every current design theme and avoided all of them.

Block Branding extended the brewery's hands-on approach to their labels. The design process began with a $50 photocopier and ended with packaging and advertising just as "ballsy" as the brand it represented.

Four In Hand • *Novato, California, USA* • *Design by Stranger & Stranger*

Brouwerij 't IJ

AMSTERDAM, NETHERLANDS • DESIGN BY POSITIVITY

After a tour of US microbreweries, Brouwerij 't IJ came home to Amsterdam with a taste for West Coast IPAs and East Coast street art. They went to work on this grassy, citrusy IPA and handed a four-word creative brief to the designer. "Tits, tattoos, and skulls" was the only directive for this tongue-in-cheek, punk rock label.

The label is quite a departure from the rest of the IJ lineup, which feature traditionally designed die-cut labels. Their ostrich and egg logo is carried over here, though in tattoo form this time.

Bomb Beer Co.

NEW YORK, NEW YORK, USA • DESIGN BY BILLY THE ARTIST

Bomb Beer Company identified New York City's starving artists, gamers and hipsters as their market. To reach this demographic, the brewery focused on keeping the beer affordable, offering "craft beer without craft beer prices." In order to visually appeal to this younger, alternative demographic, Bomb Lager turned to Billy The Artist for their graffiti-inspired cans. The owners had long admired murals of his in their neighborhood. When they were introduced to Billy at a favorite bar of both of theirs, they knew he was the right fit to create their brand.

Loveland Aleworks

LOVELAND, COLORADO, USA • DESIGN BY MANUAL

This microbrewery's identity roots itself in the history of its home. Loveland, Colorado, was founded in 1877 shortly after the completion of the Colorado Central Railroad. The city took the name of William A. H. Loveland, president of the railroad. Rather than creating a gimmicky, vintage, train-centric brand, Manual chose a much more modern route, working in historical allusions along the way.

A key element of the branding is the custom typeface, which includes an inline style. Its parallel lines are a simple, yet striking connection to those original railway tracks. Mountainous shapes atop the logo recognize Loveland's location as a gateway to Rocky Mountain National Park.

The tap handles are modeled after 19th century railroad signal levers. The rest of the Loveland tap room seamlessly incorporates reclaimed materials into a clean and modern setting.

Monteith's Single Source • Greymouth, New Zealand • Design by Designworks

Dykes Brewery

ALNÖ, SWEDEN · DESIGN BY SARAH COLOBONG

Despite opening in 2013, the history of Dykes Brewery starts fifty years earlier when co-founder Dick Dykes began brewing beer at the age of eleven in England. Dick moved to Sweden in 1975, but quickly found himself missing English ales. He began brewing to satisfy his own appetite. In 1985 he empowered others to do the same, opening one of the country's first homebrew supply stores. The next step was opening Dykes Brewery with his son Robert.

For the labels, Swiss designer Sarah Colobong takes a decidedly minimal approach. Her art is balanced and restrained, just like the beer they represent. Water is the most important ingredient for the brewery as well as the designer. Dykes utilizes some of Europe's highest-quality water, sourcing it from nearby Sundsvall. Each label features a geometric pattern representing water in its three stages: solid, liquid, and gas. As a final touch, each label is hand stamped with Dykes' "Modern Tradition" tagline.

Ippon Matsu

NEW YORK, NEW YORK, USA • DESIGN BY KOTA KOBAYASHI

In 2011 a savage tsunami crashed down upon the city of Rikuzentakata, Japan, claiming 1,700 lives. The devastation was especially visible at the Takata-Matsubara. This stretch of forest along the coast was home to 70,000 pine trees. After the tsunami, however, just a single 200-year-old pine remained. This surviving tree has become a national symbol of hope.

Kota Kobayashi is a Japanese designer living in New York City. He created Ippon Matsu to help the recovery process in his home country. Profits from the beer sales are donated to businesses in Rikuzentakata affected by the disaster.

"Ippon Matsu" translates to "One Pine Tree." Handwritten seals atop each beer tell the story behind it. The upward-facing triangles of the label's tree point toward recovery and a brighter future.

Harbour Brewing Co. • Bodmin, Cornwall, England • Design by A-Side Studio

New Belgium Brewing

FORT COLLINS, COLORADO, USA • DESIGN BY HATCH

New Belgium's logo started in 1989 with founder Jeff Lebesch's vacation spent biking to various Belgian breweries. The homebrewer returned to Colorado inspired and created the recipe that would become Fat Tire Amber Ale. It was a great success, but consumers were not identifying New Belgium as the brewer of Fat Tire. Cultivator Advertising & Design created a new logo to restore that connection, tying together the brand name, flagship beer and brewery's history. New Belgium has gone on to become the fourth largest craft brewery in the United States and have recently opened a brewery in Asheville, North Carolina. Their high levels of success, however, have not kept them from looking to improve their brand.

In 2014 design firm Hatch refreshed the logo, increasing the contrast and swapping out the Copperplate Gothic type that has become quite popular with breweries. The firm redesigned the entire New Belgium portfolio, unifying the offerings visually to encourage their customers to explore beyond the very successful Fat Tire. The brewery name is much more prominent on the packaging, further connecting the individual beers with the company. One element they did retain was the playful watercolors that have always been a central part of the New Belgium brand. These had always flowed from the brush of founder Kim Jordan's neighbor Ann Fitch, until her recent retirement. Artist Leah Giberson picked up where Anne left off, creating new renditions that continue the spirit of the brewery while adding a splash of Americana.

Great Divide Brewing Co. • Denver, Colorado, USA • Design by Cultivator Advertising & Design

Brouwerij Bosteels

BUGGENHOUT, BELGIUM • DESIGN BY ANTOINE BOSTEELS

Beer styles continue to expand and demonstrate that they are much more than fizzy, yellow, and brewed to pair with an afternoon spent on a lawn mower. DeuS is a Bière de Champagne—a relatively new beer style whose brewing process has many similarities to the way in which champagne is made. Many of these beers are even transported to the Champagne region of France to undergo the "Methode Champagnoise" phases of secondary fermentation and storage. Due to their high level of carbonation they are also found in thick champagne-style bottles complete with a cork and cage topper.

Brouwerij Bosteels' DeuS and Infinium are two highly rated examples of the Bière de Champagne style, found in sophisticated packaging suitable for the champagne shelf.

Samuel Adams

BOSTON, MA, USA • DESIGN BY THE BOSTON BEER COMPANY

Released prior to Christmas, Samuel Adams' Infinium presents itself as the perfect toasting beer to bring in the New Year. Brewed in collaboration with the oldest brewery in the world, Germany's Weihenstephan, this beer is billed as the first new beer style created under the Reinheitsgebot in over a hundred years. Staying within these five hundred year old confines produced an innovative high-alcohol, champagne-like beer.

Harviestoun Brewery

ALVA, SCOTLAND • DESIGN BY THREEBRAND

"Ola Dubh" (pronounced 'ola doo') is Gaelic for "black oil." This beer is created by aging their chocolatey, award-winning Old Engine Oil black ale in barrels that previously housed Highland Park 12 Year Old Single Malt Whisky. Each limited release bottle is signed, dated and numbered.

The Orkney Brewery

SANDWICK, SCOTLAND • DESIGN BY GOOD CREATIVE

Located in a former schoolhouse, the Orkney Brewery creates award-winning beer from the Neolithic Orkney Islands in Scotland. (Thus the tagline "5,000 Years in the Making.") Dark Island Reserve is the result of aging their Dark Island Ale in whisky barrels for three months. They are hand labeled, numbered and signed by head brewer Andrew Fulton. Each limited-edition bottle features an etching of the famous Orkney Standing Stones.

Brewers & Union • Cape Town, South Africa • Designed by Collective São Gabriel

Choc Beer • Krebs, Oklahoma, USA • Designed by Funnel Design Group

Monsieur Gordo • Madrid, Spain • Design by LOLA

Mateo & Bernabé and Friends

LOGROÑO, SPAIN • DESIGN BY MORUBA

Logroño is the capital of the autonomous community of La Rioja in northern Spain. This region is known for its wine, which is an important component of their economy. In 2012, Mateo & Bernabé began making the first hand-crafted beer in La Rioja. The brewery and its beers draw their names from the city's patrons saints.

Mateo draws its name from the patron saint of Logroño's wine harvest festival. This weeklong event begins the Saturday before September 21st, which is the day of the feast of San Mateo. The prominent "21" on the beer's label marks this date. The traditional tool used for harvesting grapes, the corquete, is also featured on the bottle. Fittingly for a beer from a region famous for its wine, Mateo is a wheat ale with strong, fruity tones.

The Bernabé label dates back to 1521, when the French under King Francis I crossed into Spain and held Logroño under siege. Fish caught in the Ebro River kept the people alive until the French besiegers were finally fought off on June 11th. This date is now celebrated as the feast of San Bernabé, the city's patron saint. This sweet, fruity, and fish-clad golden ale bears his name.

Santiago is a Belgian-style abbey ale. It is numbered for Saint James' Day, celebrated annually on July 25th. Saint James was one of Jesus' first disciples and his remains are believed to be buried at the spot of the Cathedral of Santiago de Compostela Galicia in northwest Spain. Many make the pilgrimage along the Camino de Santiago (or Way of Saint James) to visit this shrine, a route which passes through Logroño. The scallop shell has become a metaphor for these travelers. Just as the ocean waves push these shells to the beaches of Galicia, God guides these pilgrims to Santiago. The grooves of the shell also represent travelers from various homes converging on this singular location.

The Running of the Bulls is part of the eight day festival in Pamplona celebrating Saint Fermín. The celebrations span July 6-14, with the first bull running held on July 7. Most runners wear the traditional white shirt and pants with a red waistband and neckerchief. So this well-balanced red ale fits right in with the dress code. Fermín's prominent malts ensure it will be much sweeter than the bulls of Pamplona.

Shepherd Neame Generation Ale • *Faversham, Kent, England* • *Design by Stuart Adams*

Almanac Beer Co.

SAN FRANCISCO, CALIFORNIA, USA • DESIGN BY DAMIAN FAGAN

Founders Jesse Friedman and Damian Fagan met at a San Francisco homebrew club. Jesse was immediately impressed with the labels Damian had created for his beers, thinking that they were from a commercial brewery he had not yet discovered. The two bonded over their passion for brewing (and Damian's obsession for designing labels) and opened Almanac Beer Co. in the Dogpatch neighborhood in 2010.

The name is derived from the *Farmers' Almanac*, which serves as a seasonal agricultural record. Jesse and Damian create small batch beers inspired by local produce. They partner with a local farm and brew according to what is in season. Thus their brewing record serves as an archive of California seasons past. Damian's finely crafted labels certainly convey the company's "farm-to-barrel" spirit.

Jesse and Damian began brewing with fresh, local blackberries with Almanac's first beer. For their spring 2014 release they went back to the bush. Farmer's Reserve Blackberry is a sour blonde ale loaded with fruit from Swanton Berry Farm before aging in wine barrels.

The fragrant zest of Buddha's Hand citrons collides with tart bergamot oranges in their Farmer's Reserve Citrus. This cask-aged sour blonde ale was Almanac's summer 2014 release and pairs perfectly with sushi.

Before Silicon Valley was Silicon Valley, it was poetically known as the Valley of The Heart's Delight. Nonprofit Garden to Table hand-picked apricots for this beer, which supports the organization's urban farming objective. This sour ale was first released in February 2014, making a curtain call one year later.

In March 2015, Farmer's Reserve Strawberry hit shelves after its time in barrels. This beer showcases strawberries from Dirty Girl Farms in the Santa Cruz Mountains. These fruits give the ale a prominent tartness as well as a bit of a red hue. This ale can be enjoyed all summer long, or left to age in the bottle for a future harvest.

Almanac's Fresh Beer Limited Series • *Design by Damian Fagan*

Almanac's Fresh Beer Series • *Lettering by Erik Marinovich*

Russell Brewing Company • Surrey, British Columbia, Canada • Design by Atmosphere Design

Moa Brewing Co.

MARLBOROUGH, NEW ZEALAND • DESIGN BY ONE DESIGN

Moa founder and head brewer Josh Scott is the son of a winemaker and incorporates some of those techniques into his brewing process. Scott is also a cyclist competing for a position on the national squad. He found a way to incorporate this into his brewery as well. In 2012 Moa upset larger competitors and took over as the official beer of the New Zealand Olympic teams. Clearly motivated by the top-quality design work, the Kiwis had one of their most successful Olympic games that summer in London.

They flew home with six gold, two silver and five bronze medals. This partnership continued at the Sochi 2014 Winter Olympics and will again in Rio in 2016.

One Design dug deep into the Bridgeman Archive for Moa's Olympic beer packaging. These vintage bare-knuckle fighters add plenty of history (and silly pants) to the packaging. Their work also made an appearance on the medal stand in 2012, taking home gold at the Brew NZ Awards.

Het Anker

MECHELEN, BELGIUM • DESIGN BY DE BEMANNING

The term "Maneblusser" translates to "moon extinguisher" and is an endearing name used for the locals of Mechelen, Belgium. The term dates back to the night of January 27, 1687, when fog engulfed Saint Rumbold's tower. A jolly bar patron glanced upon the cathedral as the moon's glow illuminated the fog with a red hue. His drunken eyes deceived him as he screamed, "Fire, fire, the tower is on fire!" Locals sounded the alarm and ran to help extinguish the blaze. Their assistance proved unnecessary, as the moon moved away from tower, putting out the "flames" for them.

The label of this Belgian pale ale depicts a jovial Maneblusser carrying beer in his water bucket. It also proudly wears the red and yellow colors of the Mechelen city flag.

Fullsteam Brewery

DURHAM, NC, USA • DESIGN BY HELMS WORKSHOP

Durham's Fullsteam Brewery has created a distinctively Southern beer culture in this once-booming tobacco town. Their "plow to pint" brews utilize produce from local farmers and are intended to pair well with Southern cuisine. Ingredients include local honey, sweet potatoes, basil, persimmons, pears, chestnuts, and figs. The vintage packaging from Helms Workshop wraps their brews in Southern heritage.

Austin Beerworks

AUSTIN, TEXAS, USA • DESIGN BY HELMS WORKSHOP

No mountain streams, no illustrated hops, and no barley stalks will be found on these labels. Instead, Helms Workshop focused on what made this brewery special and created a brand around it that would make their beer stand out on the shelves.

Helms began working with the four founders of Austin Beerworks very early in the process, before they had a name or even a brewery. The group noted that none of the city's eight breweries claimed the name "Austin." Marrying their brand with this iconic, eclectic, and creative city, Austin Beerworks was born.

For the brand's visuals, they ran far, far away from norms of the cooler shelves. They instead concentrated on the bold, crisp beers and quirky personalities that comprised the company. The resulting cans are a proud, strong, and uncluttered oasis. The beer names come from unique sources including Norse mythology, power tools, and 1980s action movies.

OTHER
HALF

GREEN
DIAMONDS

IMPERIAL IPA   9.1% ABV   1 PT. (16 FL OZ)

Other Half Brewing Company • Brooklyn, New York, USA • Design by Small Stuff

No-Li Brewhouse

SPOKANE, WASHINGTON, USA • DESIGN BY RILEY CRAN

After their contact attempts to a similarly named brewery were ignored, Northern Lights Brewing Co. decided to rebrand as No-Li Brewhouse. Pronounced No Lie, the new name also serves as "a subtle nod to how they candidly brew their beers and run their business."

The lack of response they received from the other brewery lives on through their Silent Treatment Pale Ale.

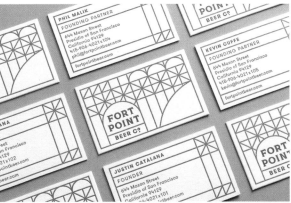

Fort Point Beer Co.

SAN FRANCISCO, CALIFORNIA, USA • DESIGN BY MANUAL

The inspiration for Fort Point's packaging and branding comes from the brewery's location. They operate out of a historic Presidio building near Fort Point National Historic Site. This fort was built right before the Civil War, protecting the bay from water attack.

The clean, classic lines spanning the visual brand are a nod to another neighbor of theirs, the Golden Gate Bridge. This relationship is further enforced with the use of gold foil throughout their labels and visual brand. This accent adds sophistication to an already crisp and modern brand. The angled serifs of the logotype are a perfect match for the architecture-inspired line art.

FORT POINT

Vocation Brewery • Hebden Bridge, England • Design by Robot Food

Copper Kettle Brewing

DENVER, COLORADO, USA • DESIGN BY EMRICH OFFICE

For this beer, Copper Kettle Brewing Company found inspiration in a 500 year old Aztec recipe for Mexican hot chocolate. Brewing ingredients include bittersweet chocolate, red Mexican chili peppers, and ground cinnamon. Within Copper Kettle's first year, this stout won a gold medal at the Great American Beer Festival in the Herb & Spice beer category.

The foil labels are printed with a copper ink and feature a custom-made Aztec cacao god. Designer Josh Emrich blends imagery and motifs from the Toltec, Aztec, and Mayan cultures to complete this label.

Researchers now believe that chocolate was invented accidentally—and we have beer to thank for it. In the late 1990s, archaeologists found traces of cacao on ancient Honduran brewing pottery fragments dating back 3,000 years. This discovery makes chocolate 500 years older than previously believed. At that time, South American beer makers unknowingly created chocolate as a by-product of the brewing process. They fermented cacao seedpods, using the pod pulp for their batch of beer (known as "chicha") and the seeds were then discarded. Eventually, they discovered the chocolate that they had created in the fermented cacao seeds. Chocolate quickly became wildly popular. Later, these ancient brewers would begin grinding up the fermented cacao seeds and adding them to the beer as a thickening agent.

The Maya and the Aztec both believed that chocolate was created by the gods and handed down to man. A hot, non-alcoholic chocolate drink was especially treasured and only allowed to be consumed by elite and royal men.

Chocolate was used in religious ceremonies (including weddings and baptisms) as well as for a wide variety of medicinal uses. Yearly festivals paid tribute to the cacao god. Cacao seeds would even become a common currency throughout Mesoamerica before the Spanish conquest.

7 | Innovation

The growth of craft beer has sparked further experimentation. Brewers are pushing the boundaries of their profession, creating exciting and unique offerings. Alcohol contents are skyrocketing, new ingredients are embraced, and traditional styles are being pushed well past the breaking point. You do not need to look too far to find a beer that spent two months at sea or one whose ingredients include beef jerky, donuts, bull testicles, or beard hair.

This creativity on the brewing end has been coupled with packaging just as inventive. Traditional packaging elements are becoming less common. Designers are no longer starting with a common bottle and a paper label displaying the beer and brewery name. New containers are being invented and alternate label materials are being put to use for beers to stand out from the crowd. Breweries are going as far as incorporating taxidermy into their packaging, with no signs of slowing down.

Mikkeller

COPENHAGEN, DENMARK • DESIGN BY BEDOW

In 2012, famed collaborator Mikkeller worked with Swedish design firm Bedow for four seasonal releases. The labels for each limited-edition beer were printed with heat-sensitive ink, such that the labels' scenes change as the bottles get warmer.

For the Pale Spring Ale, the snowflake turns into a sun. As the Summer Pilsner warms, the bud turns into a flower. Dandelion seeds become raindrops on the Autumn Porter. Finishing out the series, and the calendar year, the Wild Winter Ale shows an apple tree losing its leaves.

Wiper and True

BRISTOL, ENGLAND • DESIGN BY STUDIOMAKGILL

In order to make beer, brewers go through a process of turning natural ingredients into a new and exciting product. This concept is central to the Wiper and True brand. Design firm StudioMackgill wanted to look at this process from a different angle. Their label illustrations depict other examples of man's ability to tame nature and turn it into something remarkable. Note the six-pointed brewer's stars that accompany each icon.

These characters come to life in foil on the Wiper and True labels. In order to reduce printing costs, the gold foil effect was actually produced by printing cyan and magenta on silver foil. It was a focus of StudioMackgill's to stay away from the extremely masculine labels that are so common. The label's strong yet stylish typography achieves this gender-neutral goal. Visually, the Wiper and True lineup certainly strengthens their "No ordinary beer" tagline.

BrewDog

ELLON, SCOTLAND • TAXIDERMY BY TONY ARMITSTEAD

In 2010, Scotland's BrewDog grabbed headlines by releasing the highest alcohol content beer on record—and they put it in roadkill. Seven stoats and four grey squirrels, if we want to be precise. Aside from weighing in at 55% ABV, this freeze-distilled Belgian blond ale also set the record for the highest-priced beer at about $750 per bottle.

The End of History is not a foreshadowing of what will happen to your memory after drinking a beer of this strength. But rather, it is an ode to political scientists Francis Fukuyama's famous 1989 essay (and subsequent book). In his work, Fukuyama argued that Western liberal democracy was the end of the evolutionary road and thus "the end of history."

BrewDog declared this beer to be the end of their quest to redefine the limits of modern brewing. In their quest to push the boundaries further than ever before, they also created the 41% Sink the Bismarck as well as the 32% Tactical Nuclear Penguin.

Incredibly, the End of History is not their only foray into the world of taxidermy beer packaging. In 2011 they released Ghost Deer, a 28% blonde ale which was only available dispensed from the mouth of a mounted deer head.

As you might expect, BrewDog has received their share of criticism for their high-octane releases. The brewery's response was a 0.5% ABV release named "Nanny State."

Spruce Tip Stout

VANCOUVER, CANADA • DESIGN BY SAINT BERNADINE

In honor of 2013 British Columbia Craft Beer Month, R&B Brewing, Brassneck Brewery, Red Truck Brewing, Main Street Brewing, and 33 Acres Brewing gathered for a special collaboration. Like a scout troop these five breweries set out into the wilderness collecting fresh spruce tips for their brew. Not wanting the work to go unrewarded, design firm Saint Bernadine embroidered a merit badge to mark the achievement.

Celebrants of BC Craft Beer Month were also able to earn this badge. Their only requirement was to find and enjoy this light-bodied stout in the wild. The label easily peels off as a keepsake.

Viru

TARTU, ESTONIA • DESIGN BY BRAND MANUAL

It is not every day—or maybe any day—that you see an eight-sided beer bottle. Viru, named after the independent country Virumaa in ancient Estonia, wears the unique shape well. Their octagonal pyramid bottles were inspired by the medieval towers of Tallinn, Estonia's capital city. The unusually small label and simplified graphics draw further attention to the contemporary bottle, making it the focus of the brand. The blue, black, and white company colors come from the nation's flag known as *sinimustvalge* ("blue-black-white"). Just above the logo and embossed at the bottom of the bottle are the words *"Oled see, mida jood"* which translates to "You are what you drink." If you are drinking Viru, you are getting a bright 5% ABV pilsner brewed with Lithuanian barley, Saaz hops and water sourced from the brewery's artesian well.

Samuel Adams

BOSTON, MASSACHUSETTS, USA • THE BOSTON BEER CO.

The Boston Beer Company has been tinkering with extreme beers for decades. Their first such release was their 17.5% ABV Triple Bock. Debuting in 1994, this beer set the record for the strongest beer ever brewed. It also marked the first time a beer was aged in liquor barrels, a practice that is now commonplace with so many brewers.

In 2002 the brewery unveiled Utopias, a 24% ABV uncarbonated strong ale meant to be enjoyed at room temperature. This port-like $200 beer would not be served properly from a stock beer bottle. Instead, Samuel Adams did it service with a lavish resealable ceramic decanter. The gold accents harken back to a time were the elite drank from vessels emblazoned with gold and jewels. To remind you that it is beer after all, they cleverly shaped the bottle to resemble a brew kettle.

Maria's Packaged Goods & Community Bar

CHICAGO, ILLINOIS, USA • DESIGN BY FRANKLYN

Kaplan's Liquors first opened in Chicago in 1939. Despite the long history, locals began calling it by another name soon after Maria Marszewski took over as owner in 1986. When she handed the reins to her sons in 2010, they officially renamed the business "Maria's Packaged Goods & Community Bar."

The rebranding effort was handled by Michael Freimuth. He created a unique packaging and identity system for this rather unique establishment. Maria's had evolved into a liquor store with a neighborhood bar located behind an unmarked door. Aside from the hundreds of craft beers in stock, as well as their famous "$2 random shitty beer," they have also added craft beer offerings of their own to the shelves.

Beers in paper bags have been carried out of liquor stores for decades, but never have they been so well crafted. Brown bags have been discarded for well-tailored white paper, adorned with custom stamps and handdrawn type.

Longwood Brewery

NANAIMO, CANADA • DESIGN BY HIRED GUNS CREATIVE

The deep, dark color of this Russian imperial stout inspired Longwood Brewery to take its packaging into outer space. This brew features an unusual black matte bottle. The bold prismatic foil lettering leaps off of the overwhelmingly dark backdrop. The label also features subtle embossing that tells the story of the beer in Morse code.

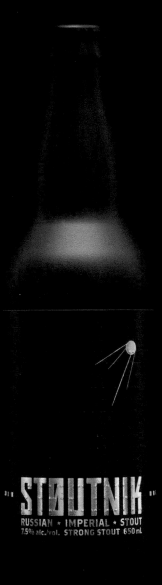

STØUTNIK

RUSSIAN ★ IMPERIAL ★ STOUT
7.5% alc./vol. STRONG STOUT 650 mL

Sly Fox Brewing Co.

POTTSTOWN, PA, USA • DESIGN BY VIRTUAL FARM CREATIVE

The beer can has seen many iterations since its inception in 1935. Changes have slowed down as of late. The last two notable modifications have been the stay-tab, introduced in 1975, and the wide-mouth opening, which was ushered in by Coors in 1997.

Crown Holdings, inventor of the modern bottle cap, decided it was time to once again revisit the currently accepted beer can design. They developed the 360 End® can, whose entire lid peels off. This opening mechanism creates a much larger opening, closer mimicking the experience of drinking from a glass.

In 2013, Sly Fox Brewing began packaging their Helles Golden Lager in these peel-off cans, becoming the first North American brewery to do so. Sly Fox has established themselves as much more than a gimmick, winning GABF gold medals for their Pikeland Pils, Rauchbier, and 360 IPA Grisette.

Omnipollo

STOCKHOLM, SWEDEN • DESIGN BY KARL GRANDIN

There are a few things you assume every beer label will contain: brewery name, brewery logo, and the name of the beer. Karl Grandin made a lot of distributors sweat by throwing all of these out the window on the way to creating a wonderfully bizarre, and oddly cohesive, collection of labels. As Grandin explains, "Most of the Omnipollo images come from daydreams and I try to bring that psychedelic logic into the artwork. It's a universe that is slowly growing, forming a world of far out environments, characters, and symbols, one bottle at a time."

Austin Beerworks

AUSTIN, TEXAS, USA • DESIGN BY HELMS WORKSHOP

Let me introduce you to seven feet, eighty-six pounds of history. Austin Beerworks and Helms Workshop have been working together since the brewery was merely a glimmer in Adam, Will, Mike, and Michael's collective eye. It is one of those relationships where two plus two equals ten thousand. As is typical in the design world, the client had a problem. Peacemaker Extra-Pale Ale was not performing as well as expected. Consumers were finding the "extra pale" classification confusing.

The first step of Helms' solution was renaming the beer "Anytime Ale." The new name clearly implies that this is a light, easy-drinking beer that isn't so strong that you'll be

displaying your karaoke version of "Pour Some Sugar on Me" after three or four. They then created the world's first and only 99-pack.

In case you needed help finding an excuse, the mammoth packaging lists occasions that are the perfect time for an Anytime Ale. These include "You wanna out-recycle the neighbors," "Non-video conference call," "Reading the terms & conditions," and "Long line at the bank."

8 | Homebrew Labels

The attention paid to beer packaging has clearly grown exponentially. Macro- and microbrewers alike are allotting more resources into their visual brand than ever before. One unforeseen result of this progression is its effect on homebrewing. These kitchen crafters have long been working hard to create beer of professional quality, often dissecting their favorite beers in a quest to replicate them. Some of these homebrewers are now putting just as much effort into labels that look like they belong next to them on the store shelf. One homebrewer in particular has gone as far as to hire a design firm to create custom letterpress labels for his operation.

Hummm n' Hammer

CHARLOTTE, NC, USA • DESIGN BY SHEA STEWART

Cerveja Tupã

SÃO PAULO, BRAZIL • DESIGN BY DAVID MICHELSOHN

One Small Step IPA

LONDON, ENGLAND • DESIGN BY JOSH SMITH

Bear Flavored Ales

BEACON, NEW YORK, USA • DESIGN BY DEREK DELLINGER

Academic Brewery

GAINESVILLE, FLORIDA USA • DESIGN BY DERRICK LIGON

You Rock!

THE HAGUE, NETHERLANDS • DESIGN BY PATSWERK

To celebrate their 7th anniversary, the fine folks at Patswerk decided to create a special gift for their clients and friends. Each gift box contains an IPA, a porter, and a glass. Both beers were brewed by Patswerk and silk-screened with their skillful icon design.

The Fermentation Society

RICHMOND, VIRGINIA, USA • DESIGN BY WORK LABS

Design studio WORK Labs has teamed up with local homebrewers. When members brew a new batch, they register it online. They are then sent caps and labels with a unique QR code. As they hand out their product, people can scan the label, go online, and give the beer a review.

Roscoe's Fine Ale

PORTLAND, OREGON, USA • DESIGN BY HUB COLLECTIVE

It is not uncommon for a homebrewer to invest in equipment that will set their operation apart from that of their peers. It is uncommon, however, for that equipment to include a letterpress. HUB Collective took Roscoe's homebrews to the next level with beautifully detailed let-terpress labels with a distinct look and feel. These labels are beautiful and also practical as available space provides an area for Roscoe to write the type of beer, alcohol per volume, and bottling date. While they were at it, HUB expanded the brand to shirts and posters.

Junction Brewing

MINNEAPOLIS, MINNESOTA, USA • DESIGN BY MATT ERICKSON

Dockside Brewing Co.

CINCINNATI, OHIO, USA • DESIGN BY LANDOR

Juggernaut design firm Landor has done work for some of the world's largest beer brands. A few employees at the Cincinnati office decided to take market research even further. They cleared space near the loading dock and began brewing their own creations. As expected they rolled out a fully executed brand complete with cans that depict the flavors awaiting inside the container.

List of Breweries

Photo Credits